W9-CUC-089

A

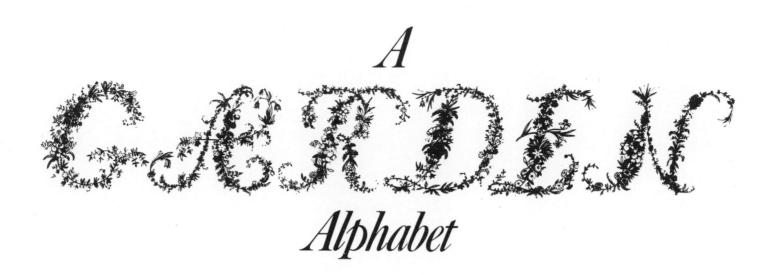

GARDEN

Alphabet

Compiled by John Harris
in association with

The Victoria and Albert Museum

for
The Garden Exhibition

Octopus Books Limited
in association with
Edgeworth Press

A Garden Alphabet

researched and written
by John Harris
designed by Helen Hamlyn
Alphabet drawn by David Coster

This book contains 24 original engravings from Batty Langley's *Pomona* or *The Fruit Garden Illustrated,* first published in 1729.
Langley was a pattern book compiler whose engraved models contributed more than any other to the ornamentation of the garden, but it is often forgotten that he started life as a practical gardener and the *Pomona* is one of his earliest books.

Illustrated on the jacket and title page is a view of Painswick, Gloucestershire, from Paris Lodge, painted by Thomas Robins in 1757.

B *both* Courtesy Bodleian Library, Oxford
C *left* Courtesy British Architectural Library
right Courtesy Country Life Limited
D *right* Courtesy Mr and Mrs Paul Mellon, Upperville, U.S.A.
G *left* Kungl. Akademian for de fria Konsterna, Stockholm
right Courtesy Victoria and Albert Museum
H *right* By Gracious Permission of Her Majesty the Queen
I *left* Courtesy Buckinghamshire County Museum, Aylesbury
right Courtesy Trustees of the John Evelyn Collection, Christ Church, Oxford
J *right* Courtesy Victoria and Albert Museum
K *right* Courtesy Victoria and Albert Museum
L Courtesy Yale Center for British Art, Yale University
M *left* Courtesy British Architectural Library
N *both* Courtesy Victoria and Albert Museum
O *right* Courtesy Devonshire Collection Chatsworth. Reproduced by Permission of the Trustees of the Chatsworth Settlement

P *right* Courtesy British Architectural Library
Q *both* Courtesy British Architectural Library
R *right* Courtesy British Architectural Library
S *right* Courtesy British Architectural Library
T *left* Courtesy British Architectural Library
right Courtesy Victoria and Albert Museum
U *both* Courtesy British Architectural Library
V *left* British Architectural Library
right Cheltenham Museum and Art Gallery
W *both* British Architectural Library
X *left* By Gracious Permission of Her Majesty the Queen
right Courtesy British Architectural Library
Y *left* Courtesy of the National Trust
right Courtesy Buckinghamshire County Museum, Aylesbury
Z *left* Courtesy Royal Zoological Society, London
right Courtesy Colin Lacy Gallery Limited

First published in Great Britain in 1979 by
Octopus Books Limited
59 Grosvenor Street
London W.1.

© 1979 John Harris
ISBN 0 7064 1082 3

Produced by Edgeworth Press
Edgeworth, Nr. Stroud, Gloucestershire.

Printed in Great Britain
by William Clowes & Sons Limited

The Prospect of PAINSWICK &c in Gloss'shire
from PANS LODGE in COLBOURN-GROVE
belonging to Benjamin Hyett Esq.

Robins Pinx
1758

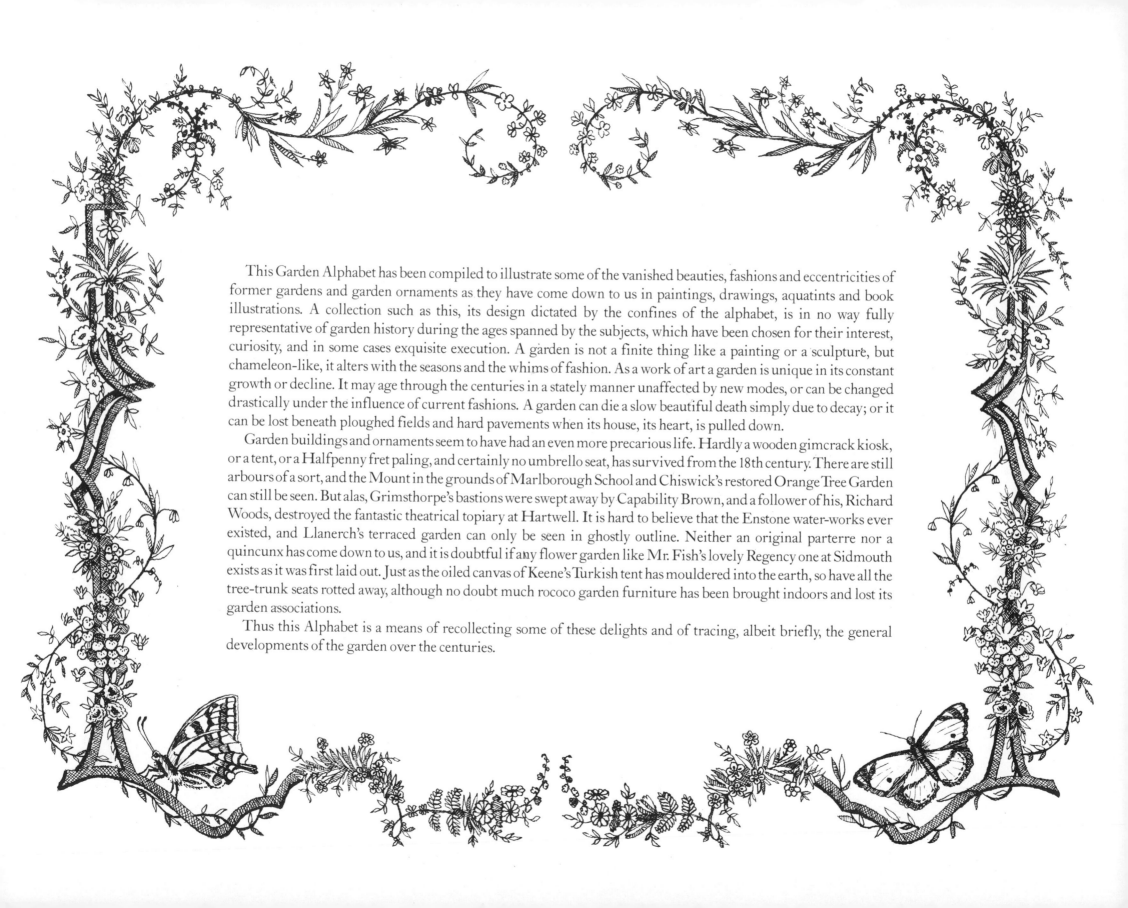

This Garden Alphabet has been compiled to illustrate some of the vanished beauties, fashions and eccentricities of former gardens and garden ornaments as they have come down to us in paintings, drawings, aquatints and book illustrations. A collection such as this, its design dictated by the confines of the alphabet, is in no way fully representative of garden history during the ages spanned by the subjects, which have been chosen for their interest, curiosity, and in some cases exquisite execution. A garden is not a finite thing like a painting or a sculpture, but chameleon-like, it alters with the seasons and the whims of fashion. As a work of art a garden is unique in its constant growth or decline. It may age through the centuries in a stately manner unaffected by new modes, or can be changed drastically under the influence of current fashions. A garden can die a slow beautiful death simply due to decay; or it can be lost beneath ploughed fields and hard pavements when its house, its heart, is pulled down.

Garden buildings and ornaments seem to have had an even more precarious life. Hardly a wooden gimcrack kiosk, or a tent, or a Halfpenny fret paling, and certainly no umbrello seat, has survived from the 18th century. There are still arbours of a sort, and the Mount in the grounds of Marlborough School and Chiswick's restored Orange Tree Garden can still be seen. But alas, Grimsthorpe's bastions were swept away by Capability Brown, and a follower of his, Richard Woods, destroyed the fantastic theatrical topiary at Hartwell. It is hard to believe that the Enstone water-works ever existed, and Llanerch's terraced garden can only be seen in ghostly outline. Neither an original parterre nor a quincunx has come down to us, and it is doubtful if any flower garden like Mr. Fish's lovely Regency one at Sidmouth exists as it was first laid out. Just as the oiled canvas of Keene's Turkish tent has mouldered into the earth, so have all the tree-trunk seats rotted away, although no doubt much rococo garden furniture has been brought indoors and lost its garden associations.

Thus this Alphabet is a means of recollecting some of these delights and of tracing, albeit briefly, the general developments of the garden over the centuries.

The Medieval garden belonged essentially to religious houses. Within its walls were walks, fountains and roses, and, of course, herbs and vegetables. In the more settled times of the Tudors many new houses and mansions which were no longer fortified, but comfortable, beautiful homes, were built in emulation of the royal ones. These all had their gardens, also reflections of royal gardens, like for instance those at Henry VIII's Whitehall, Hampton Court and Nonesuch. They were still walled and contained tightly around the house, but included designs and buildings decorated with symbolic heraldry and coats of arms. There were now mounts and elaborate pergolas, gazeboes and banqueting houses.

The Jacobean age witnessed a revolution, for whereas the Tudor garden was essentially a continuation of the medieval pattern which incorporated elements from Italy, via France, in the 17th century the Renaissance Italian garden became an overwhelming influence. Gardens incorporated grottos, waterworks and automata, and elaborate fountains. This was the age of the mannerist garden created by such designers as Salomon and Isaac de Caus and Inigo Jones, where architecture predominated and planting and flowers were of secondary consideration.

After the Restoration in 1660 exiled courtiers returned to find gardens decayed and ruined. They brought with them new ideas from France and Holland which were in any case going to replace the Italianate grotto or terraced style. Gardens were designed with avenues which led away from the house, divided up the parterres and extended beyond the cultivated areas into vistas barred by grilles. The old walled espalier garden was abandoned. This new axial style had been perfected by André le Nôtre at the French court, but the vast scale of French planting was never emulated in England, a country wary of autocracy. Far more important was the English love of trees, and their need for wood to build ships. Evelyn's *Sylva, or a discourse on forest trees* was published in 1664 as propaganda to this effect.

Too much has been made of the reaction that set in at the Revolution in 1688, for Dutch tastes were often similar to and influenced by ideas from France. There is no doubt, however, that William III introduced the fashion for topiary work in yew and box. Topiary in Oxford colleges seems to have been introduced in the 1690s, the decade when the Winchendon and Hartwell topiary gardens were planned, and by this time even a humble garden usually boasted some complex quincunx or clipped bird or animal set in a knot garden of coloured sand.

Although the story that Vanbrugh suggested a landscape painter should be consulted to lay out Blenheim in 1705 may be apocryphal, it is illustrative of the radical change that overtook gardening in England after the turn of the century. It was not only a question of 'calling in the country', to quote Pope, but daring to venture into the country

beyond the garden, so that the boundary between the two was broken down.

At Grimsthorpe in 1707 Switzer fortified his wood to provide viewing points across the deer park, and Bridgeman and Vanbrugh were experimenting with all sorts of liberalising ideas. The 1720s saw the rise of what is called the picturesque, or literary garden, and its *eminence grise* was Pope, who loved painting and gardening and said that 'all gardening is landscape painting'. He influenced William Kent in the design of many of his gardens, including Chiswick, although this particular garden was more Italian in style, for it reflected many of the notions of the ideal arcadian garden of the Renaissance and Classical Antiquity. Some gardens like Stourhead were rigidly composed according to certain pictorial principles which echoed the painting of Claude Lorrain. Others were more arbitrarily planned, examples of that 'Regular irregularity… in the rural manner' described by Batty Langley in 1728.

About this time developed a kind of whimsical garden, with temples, umbrello seats, serpentine paths, root houses and wiggly watercourses, which were often carved out of older, formal layouts. Designed for these gardens were many of Halfpenny's or Overton's kiosks and pavilions, or Wright's arbours and grottos, and such a garden was the ancestor of the *Jardin Anglo-Chinois* in France. These gardens also featured a most remarkable revival of interest in flowers, flower gardens and rosaries. Amateur gardeners like Joseph Spence, William Southcote and Wright himself initiated the planting style that eventually developed into the Gardenesque of Loudon early in the 19th century.

The natural garden probably developed out of the expansionist policies of extending gardens and parks into the surrounding country. Capability Brown made a fashion of it with his smooth curving lawns and rotund groups of trees. Gardens were no longer near the house and not everyone approved. In 1760 Sir William Chambers created a picturesque garden at Kew which was overlaid with exotica, and where flowers were predominant. William Mason created a renowned flower garden at Nuneham in 1770. These were intimations that the art of gardening would return, as it did with Humphrey Repton in the decades each side of 1800. Repton re-established the need for formality around the house, and carefully created pictured scenes, and responded to the fashion for new plants, shrubs and trees. Hence the American Garden that Repton considered an essential adjunct to his Rosary at Ashridge. At the same time J.C. Loudon's work had considerable influence; he saw the conservatory as an extension of the house or an intrusion of the garden indoors. Loudon's work is both the end of a development and the beginning of a new one. He it was who invented the word 'Gardenesque' to describe a style 'calculated for displaying the art of the gardener'. This is, after all, what gardening is all about.

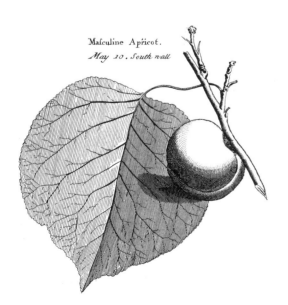

Masculine Apricot.
May 10. South wall

Apricot

...is for Arbour

These three designs for arbours were all made by Thomas Wright, who described himself 'of Durham,' and were published in 1755 in his *Universal Architecture, Book I: Six Original Designs for Arbours*. He followed this in 1758 with *Book II: Six Original Designs for Grottos*. The *Arbours* and *Grottos* have passed into history as the most beautiful and rarest of all 18th century garden pattern books. Wright, 'The Wizard of Durham,' was something of a polymath. As an astronomer he elucidated the Milky Way in 1750, and for a long time his revelations concerning the stars and planets eclipsed his earthly performances as architect and garden designer. However, he designed many Palladian houses, a dozen parkscapes, and a wild profusion of temples, kiosks, hermitages, and all sorts of garden buildings and follies before he retired to his Tullian villa near Durham. His invention was wondrous, his skill with the engraver's burin unsurpassed.

The roof of the arbour *opposite* is adorned with ornamental pineapples. Heads of muses or emperors grow from the springing of the arches and the greenery is controlled to provide hints of capitals to the columns. Arbours were built to designs such as these, but alas were ephemeral and none has survived. Like the Wizard himself, they belong to enchanted gardens now lost to us.

Black Mulberry

...is for Bastion

Here are two views by William Stukeley of the fortified wood at Grimsthorpe Castle, Lincolnshire. The plan *below* shows the fortified wood with the arrow-headed bastions pointing across the park, while the interior of one of the bastions is shown opposite.

These charming and naive drawings were made in 1736. William Stukeley was one of the most curious and beloved of all of 18th century antiquaries, and Grimsthorpe Castle would have been well-known to him as he lived in nearby Stamford. He was tireless in recording the archaeological antiquities of England, producing books on Stonehenge, Avebury and his famous travel book, the *Itinerarium Curiosum* (see M for Mount).

The remodelling of the garden at Grimsthorpe was started by Stephen Switzer for Robert Bertie, Marquess of Lindsey, in 1711. He transformed a square wood into what is virtually a fortification, whereby it was surrounded with a slightly raised terrace walk and by a concentric series of bastions pointing out across the great sweep of parkland. Switzer's idea was new at the time, as it made a visual connection between the surrounding landscape and the garden. The emulation of a military idea was deliberate, and in 17th century France military treatises were studied by great garden designers such as André le Nôtre. The most obvious example in England was Blenheim, although there the bastions were enclosed within plantations and not, as at Grimsthorpe, deliberately contrived to provide a viewing place.

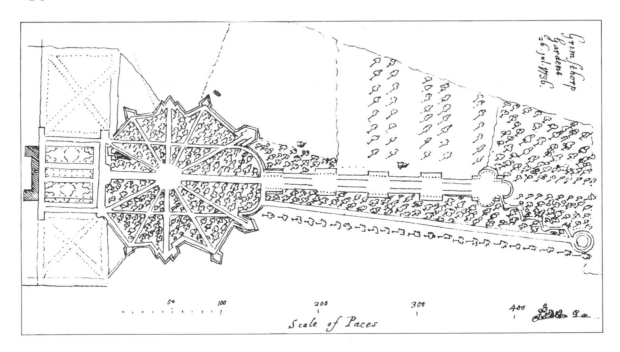

The Duchesses Bastion in Grimsthorp gardens. Aug. 10. 1736.

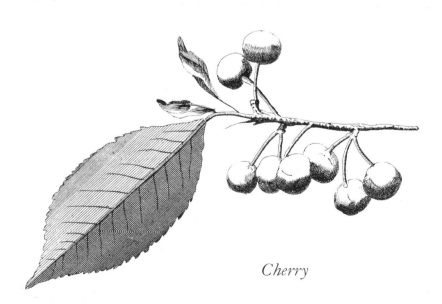

Cherry

...is for Conservatory

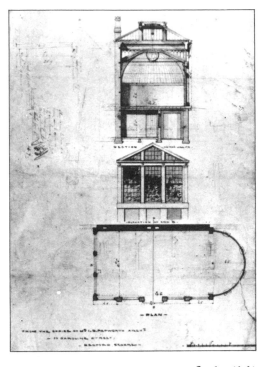

The watercolour *opposite* shows the conservatory at Capesthorne Hall, Cheshire. In 1837 E. D. Davenport summoned the architect Edward Blore to transform the 18th century Capesthorne Hall into a mansion in 'ye olden' or 'early English' style, and, as with most early Victorian mansions of this date, an attached conservatory was an essential adjunct. Capesthorne's conservatory has been attributed to Paxton, and certainly it has structural links with Paxton's Great Stove at Chatsworth begun about two years before. A contemporary definition of a conservatory as distinct from a greenhouse is given by Loudon in 1833: 'a house for keeping exotic plants, either planted in the soil, or in large tubs. When the plants are kept in flower pots on wooden stages, the house is called a greenhouse.' Both a greenhouse and an orangery (as at Hampton Court) could be an integral part of a building, and when the fashion for adding conservatories to the house died down, such areas were used as recreational extensions. The author of the *Whitsuntide Ramble to Capesthorne Park* describes the conservatory being used for Sunday School with the 'Precious truths of scripture taught amidst the fitting sights and scenes of flowers'. In most houses the conservatory was an extension of the main reception rooms on the south-east or south side of the house, and ideally led directly into the flower garden. Conservatories on the scale of this one at Capesthorne were expensive to maintain and run, and following the economic recession after the First World War, they were the first part of the country house to suffer. Thus has Paxton's Capesthorne conservatory gone the way of his Great Stove and Crystal Palace.

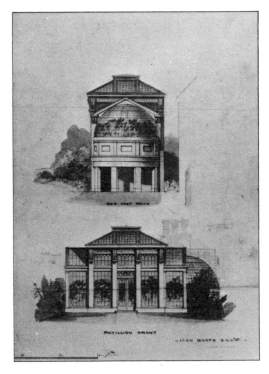

The conservatory on this page was designed for John Booth at Crouch End, Middlesex, by John B. Papworth in 1832.

Dwarf Fig

...is for Dutch Garden

This westerly view of Winchendon House and Gardens, Buckingham-shire, *opposite* was drawn in the early 18th century. The gardens at Winchendon House were celebrated as the cynosure of Dutch taste in gardening. They were laid out in the 1680s or 1690s by Thomas, 5th Baron Wharton. Winchendon was magnificently sited on the edge of the Chiltern escarpment overlooking the Vale of Aylesbury towards Waddesden. The whole garden was an elaborate exposition of complicated topiary, a fashion encouraged in England by William III and his courtiers after 1688, although there were doubtless Dutch topiary gardens before this date. As at nearby Hartwell, which dates back to Dutch William's time and is by the same designer, topiary acted like architectural trompe-l'oeil, visually linking the architecture of the house to that of the garden.

On this page is a detail of a Dutch parterre *circa* 1730.

English Warden Pear

...is for Espalier

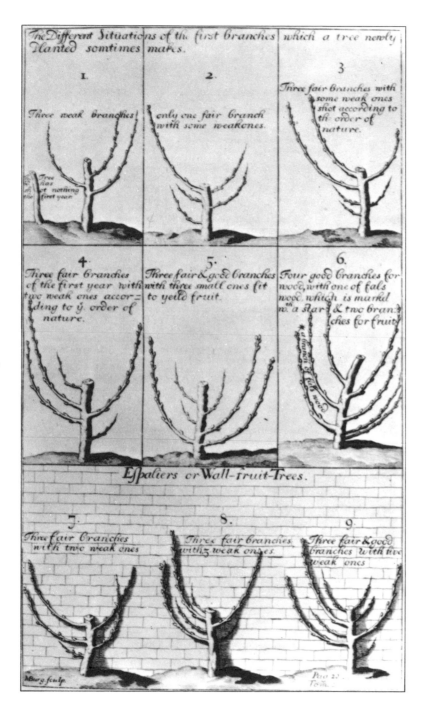

Reproduced *opposite* is an engraving of a fruit tree growing against a brick wall with horizontal 'shelters' or tiles inset in the wall. It is taken from John Lawrence's *The Clergyman's Recreation: Shewing the Pleasure and Profit of the Art of Gardening* 1715.

Espalier trees are fruit trees, usually of low growth, trained onto treillages, or framed in such a way as to make a hedge; or more commonly in the 18th century, trained onto walls of kitchen or fruit gardens. The problem with all espalier work was to force the branches to spread horizontally. Switzer in his *Ichnographia Rustica* of 1718 regarded the espalier as suitable not only to bound walks, avenues or borders, but more especially to protect plants and greens from winds. For this sort of espalier he recommended elms or limes. For fruit walls, Switzer recommends brick, 'the warmest and kindest for ripening of fruit.'

The drawing of espaliers *left* is from *The Compleat Gardener made English* by John Evelyn, 1693; a translation of *Instructions pour les Jardins Fruitiers et Potagers* of de la Quintinye.

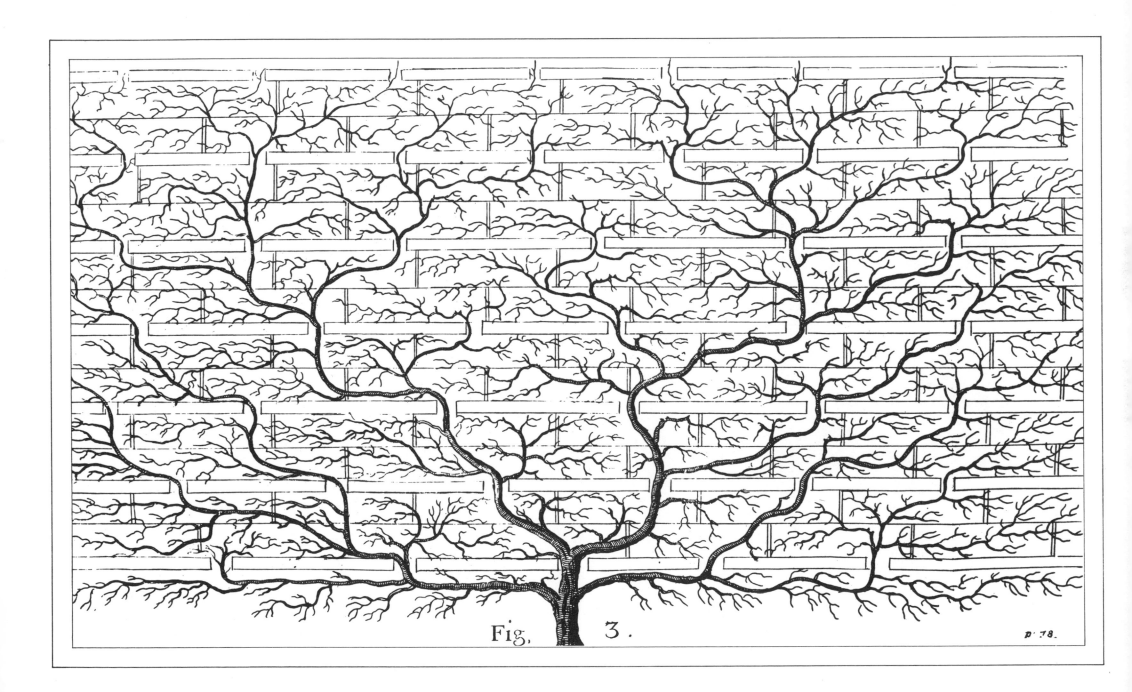

Fig. 3.

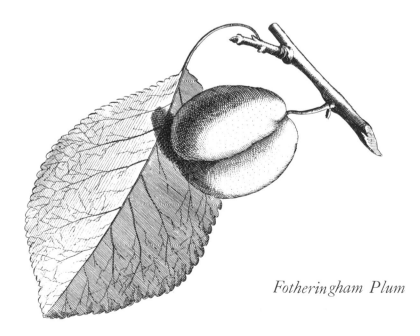

Fotheringham Plum

...is for Flower Garden

The flower garden shown on these pages is from Thomas L. Fish's elegant and now rare *Guide to Illustrations and Views of Knowle Cottage, Sidmouth*, published in 1834, the view *below* being from the drawing room into the gardens.

John Claudius Loudon, the gardening encyclopaedist of the early 19th century, extols the flower garden. For the Regency house it was the accompaniment *par excellence*, laid out on the south or south-eastern side of the house, and linked to the rooms by verandas with trellis or rustic supports entwined and garlanded with flowers and climbing creepers. Open French windows would allow the scents of the garden to pass into the principal living rooms, usually the drawing room and the library. Thomas L. Fish's Knowle Cottage at Sidmouth was a perfect example of Regency taste. It had been built by Lord Despencer in 1805, but it was Mr Fish who converted it into the 'Truly Elegant Marine Villa Ornee' after he had purchased it in 1820. His guide was published for friends and visitors staying in this fashionable seaside resort.

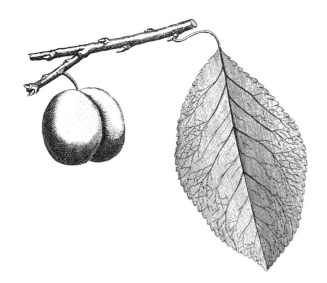

Greengage

...is for Grotto

The design for a grotto *opposite* is attributed to Isaac de Caus, the Grotto-maker.

John Woolridge's *Systema Horti-culturae: or the Art of Gardening*, produced in 1677, provided owners of 'fair Estates and Pleasant Seats' with instructions on improving their gardens. Grottos were necessary 'to repose ourselves in the time of our summer faint heats…Therefore either in the side of some decline of a Hill, or under some Mount or Terrace artificially raised, may you make a place of repose, cool and fresh in the greatest heats. It may be arched over with stone or brick and you may give it what light or entrance you please. You may make secret rooms and passages within it, and in the outer Room may you have all those before-mentioned water-works, for your own or your friends' divertisements. It is a place capable of giving you so much pleasure and delight, that you may bestow not undeservedly what cost you please on it, by paving it with Marble or immuring it with Stone or Rock-work, either Natural or Artificially resembling the excellencies of nature. The Roof may be made of the same supported with pillars of Marble, and the partitions made of Tables of the same.

The most famous of this kind that this kingdom affords is that Wiltonian Grotto near Salisbury, on which no cost was spared to make it compleat, and wherein you may view or might have lately so done the best of water-works.' The Wilton grotto was designed and constructed in the 1630s by Isaac de Caus.

The illustration on this page is a plan made by F. M. Piper in 1779 of the grotto at Stourhead, Wiltshire, built *c* 1748.

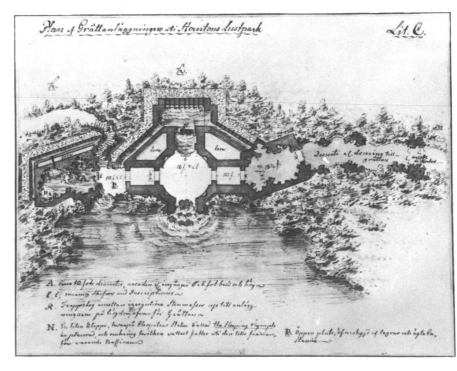

Hazelnut

...is for Hermitage

Thomas Sandby's delightful design for a Hermitage House made out of roots is shown *opposite*.

The English grafted onto the Dutch, Italian and French traditions of gardening something peculiarly English – a sense of whimsicality. No other nation ornamented their gardens with such curiosities as did the English. It was not enough just to have temples, grottos, banqueting houses or Palladian bridges, there must also be Druid's Circles, Treacle Eaters, Sugar Loaves, Jealous Walls and Egyptian Aviaries.

Thomas Sandby's hermitage or root house belongs to these creations of the make-believe. As his drawing comes from the Sandby Collection in The Royal Library, it may have been intended for the Duke of Cumberland's park at Virginia Water some time in the 1760s or 1770s.

Hermitages were meant for hermits to live in, but there were apparently few takers and fewer stayers. One hermit had to live underground, neither to be seen nor heard for seven years. The Pains Hill hermit was given a bible, hassock and mat, optical glasses and an hour glass, and instructed to stay unshaven and unclipped. He was dismissed after being found in the local pub!

Thomas Robins' drawing *above* is of Dr Jerry Pierce's Hermitage at Lilliput Castle near Bath, *circa* 1750.

Imparatrice Plum

...is for Implements

The implements shown *opposite* are John Evelyn's gardening tools as used and drawn by him *circa* 1660, from his unfinished and unpublished *Elysium Britannicum*.

The design of garden implements has changed so little that a 16th or 17th century gardener visiting a 20th century tool shed would chiefly be surprised by the innovation of stainless steel and our use of forks for digging. Tools for grafting and pruning, an important skill in the 16th century, are strikingly similar to those today. The modern gardener could do much worse than use the tools drawn by John Evelyn for his catalogue in the second book of his unpublished *Elysium Britannicum*: 'Of the Instruments belonging to a Gardiner'. The list includes the basic spades, forks, rakes, hoes, trowels and scythes, but adds surveying tools as well, for use in planning the garden. Rollers of wood or stone for grass or gravel are recommended, with a collection of knives and shears of various sizes, even 'a paire of Reachers, which are sheares fixed upon a staff'. Ladders, watering cans, syringes, pots and boxes, frames and bell-glasses are necessary, but 'a Bed-stead furnished with a tester and Curtaines of Greene . . . to draw over and preserve the choycest flowers, being in their beauty, from the parching beames of the Sunn' may seem less vital to a modern gardener. Barrows, baskets, scare-crows, and traps 'for the destruction of Birds and Vermine' are needed too, as well as labels and 'a Register or booke wherein are the names of all the flowers and plants in the Garden'.

The gardeners at work on this page were painted by B. Nebot in 1738 in the gardens of Hartwell House, Buckinghamshire.

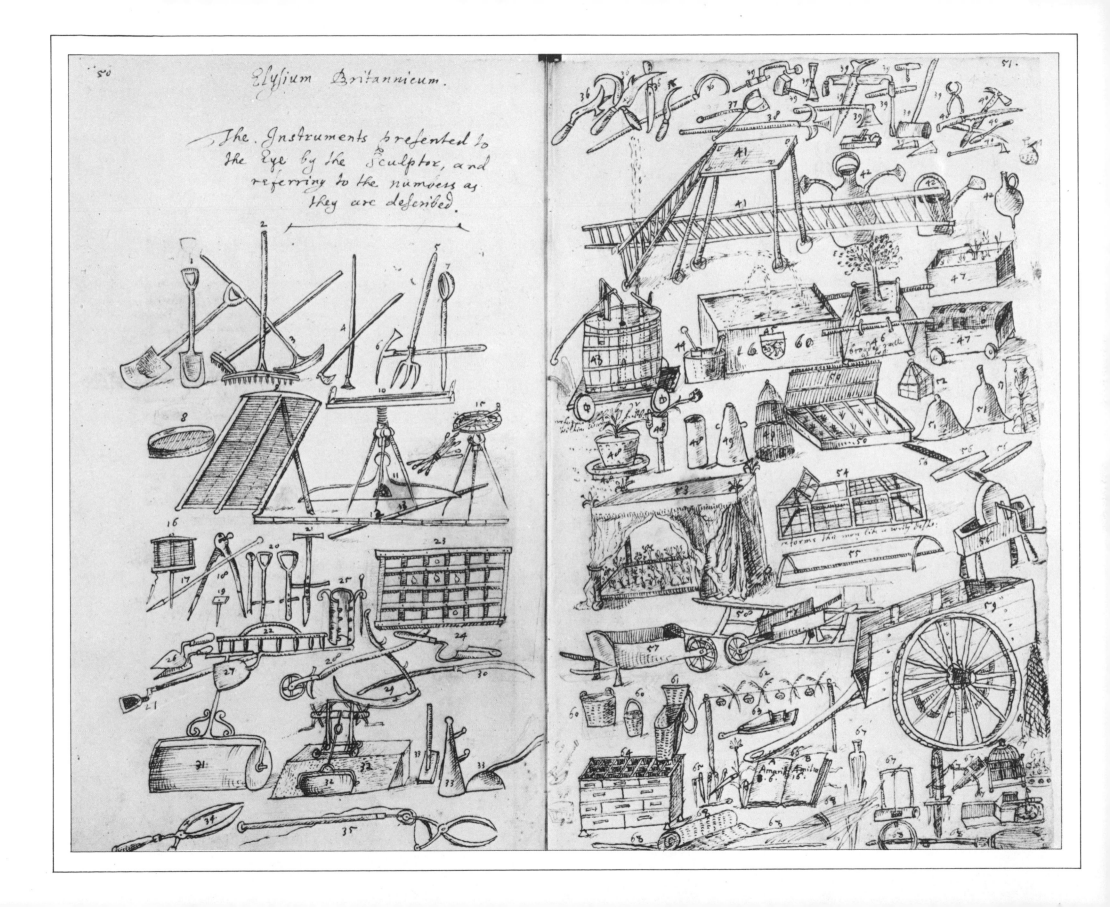

Elysium Britannicum.

The Instruments presented to
the Eye by the Sculptor, and
referring to the numbers as
they are described.

Jerusalem Apple

...is for Jardin Anglo-Chinois

The kiosk *opposite* is in the garden at Rambouillet which was ornamented for the Duc de Penthièvre in the 1770s. This engraving was published in 1784 by Le Rouge in his great survey of French gardens and garden art, *Nouveaux Jardins à la Mode*.

The Jardin Anglo-Chinois was a title which was applied to a particular type of garden in France, or to those gardens in Germany inspired by the French ones. It arose from a misunderstanding of English gardens and the belief that they imitated Chinese ones. There never was, in fact, either in France or England, any direct imitation of Chinese gardens, and the Chinese element was only present as a decorative cosmetic.

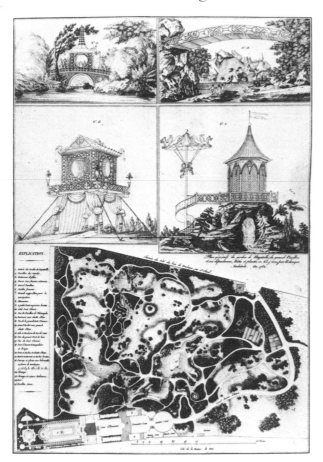

It may well have been Le Rouge who invented this description of what was at first an essentially whimsical form of English garden in the 1730s and 1740s. It was an age of grottos, cascades, fret bridges, rock gardens and other frivolous and intricate garden layouts (see X for eXotica). In the pages of Le Rouge it is possible to recognise something of the fantasy of English rococo gardens now all lost to us, as is the Chinese pavilion on its rock at Rambouillet, although the rock itself remains today. The engraving *left* shows some of the more elaborate designs conceived at this time. It was made in 1782 of the Jardin de Bagatelle which was designed and laid out by J. F. Belanger.

DES JARDINS ANGLO - CHINOIS A LA MODE.

Prix 12.ᵗᵗ

A PARIS.

Chez LE ROUGE, Ingenieur Géographe du Roi,
Rue des Grands Augustins. 1784.

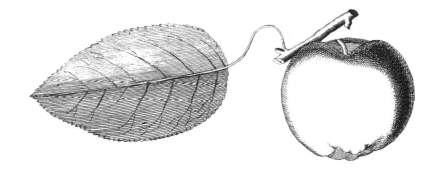

Kentish Pippin

...is for Kiosk

The composite of designs *opposite* for what Le Rouge calls 'kiosques' is really for garden temples. His title is also incorrect, since only the three-storey prospect tower *bottom left* is by William Halfpenny, the prolific pattern book compiler. The others are all from Thomas Collins Overton's *Original Designs of Temples and other Ornamental Buildings for Parks and Gardens, in the Greek, Roman and Gothic Taste* published in 1766. Overton's was a practical handbook of patterns, for at least three of his designs were used by clients near Devizes in Wiltshire. The top centre one was a temple for a Mr Richards at Spittle Croft. His designs are slightly rustic and derivative from others, especially those of Batty Langley as seen in his *Gothic Architecture Improved*, 1747. They were fashionable and almost every estate had at least one temple, perhaps by a lake for fishing or by a green for bowling, to take tea in, or simply to shelter from the sun.

This page shows a detail from Rocque's survey of Chiswick House, Middlesex, made in 1736, showing the Bagnio, the domed Orange Garden Temple (see O for Orange Tree Garden) and the Volière Garden.

Differens   Kiosques   par   Halfpenny

Lombard Pear

...is for a Lawson Garden

This picture of Llanerch, Denbighshire, dated 1662, is remarkable as the first attempt in Britain to paint a view in bird's eye perspective in oils. Wenceslaus Hollar had drawn Windsor Castle in great detail from just such an aerial position in 1659, but his drawing was not etched until later. The romantic discovery of this now vanished garden shows us the degree of elaborate formality of the gardens laid out at this time by the squirearchy even in remote parts of Wales.

The house must date from the earlier years of the 17th century and was built for Sir Peter Mutton. The garden is a perfect example of a three-tier or terrace type advocated by William Lawson in *A New Orchard and Garden* in 1597. The contrast between the stone of the house and brick of the garden walls and buildings might suggest that this garden is of later date than the house, perhaps about 1640. The two lower terraced areas are unusually complete with the extraordinary baroque curved stairs, the

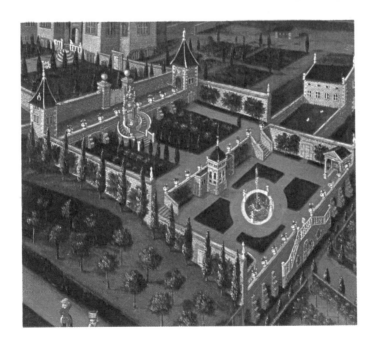

gazeboes, arbours, and lead flower pots lined on top of the walls. Most likely there was a grotto beneath the balustraded stairway of the third terrace and between the second and third terrace. The elaborate openwork building may have been a banqueting house. A cascade fills up the water storage cistern conveniently sited beside the gardener's house. The circular fountain garden dominated by Neptune may have been built later. Llanerch Mill is in the middle distance and Wrexham church on the horizon.

Medlar

...is for Mount

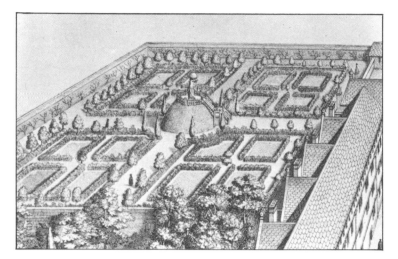

Opposite is an engraving by William Stukeley which shows the house and garden belonging to Lord Hertford. Stukeley did the sketches when he visited the house in Marlborough, Wiltshire, on the 29th June 1723. The engraving appears in his *Itinerarium Curiosum* published in 1724.

As an antiquarian interested in Stonehenge and the great mount of Silbury Hill, Stukeley was clearly fascinated by Lord Hertford's Mount. Like most other garden mounts, this one probably dates back to the 11th century and may have been the mount or motte of a Norman castle. From Elizabethan times such mounts were made into decorative features of the garden; encircling paths were cut into them, or sometimes diagonal paths as in a ziggurat. A ziggurat type of mount was constructed in New College, Oxford, in the late 17th century, and it is a self-conscious creation designed to allow the inmates to look over the college walls. The mount at Dunham Massey in Cheshire was one of Norman origin, and in this case hedges bounded the encircling paths and on the top was built a gazebo, as at Marlborough. John Leland in the 16th century remarked that mounts were furnished with topiary, with their paths 'twisting about in degrees like turning of cockleshells to come to the top without pain'. On the right of this page is a plan of Lord Hertford's garden by William Stukeley while above is the Mount with Hercules in the garden of Wadham College, Oxford, drawn and engraved by David Loggan in *Oxonia Illustrata*, 1675.

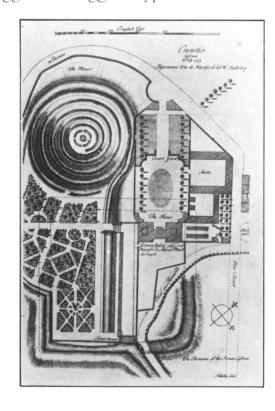

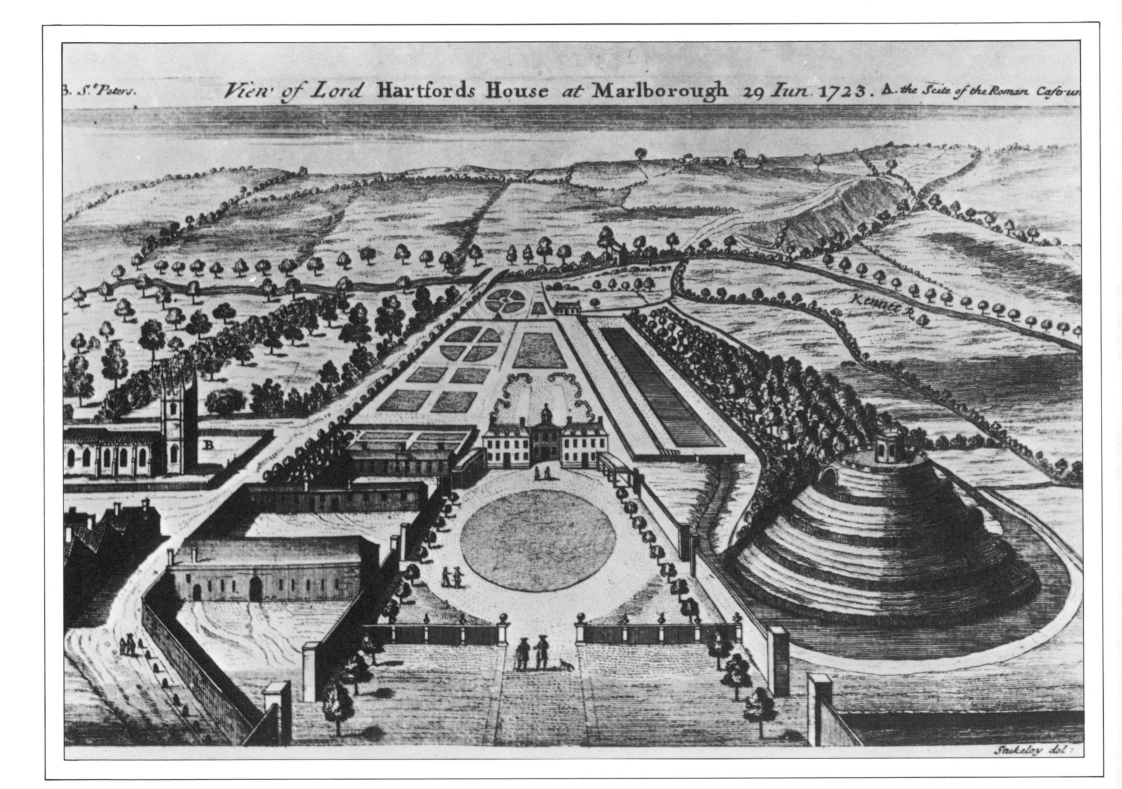

View of Lord Hartfords House at Marlborough 29 Iun. 1723. A. the Scite of the Roman Castrum. B. St Peters.

Stukeley del.

Nectarine

...is for Nurseryman's Catalogue

Robert Furber (1674-1756) founded his nursery at Kensington Gore soon after 1700. The range of exotic plants acquired from the famous gardens of Bishop Compton at Fulham Palace early established the success of his nursery. Furber was an active propagandist, publishing a catalogue of English and foreign trees in 1727, the *12 Months of Flowers* in 1730, followed by *12 Months of Fruit* in 1732, and a *Short Introduction to Gardening* in 1733. Both the Flowers and the Fruit were nurserymen's catalogues of the most lavish and beautiful kind, as Furber commissioned the emigré Antwerp painter Pieter Casteels to paint flower and fruit compositions for each month of the year.

The March selection of flowers *opposite* includes narcissi, hyacinths, tulips, anemones, maples, larch blossom, iris and cowslip, while the November selection on this page includes marigolds, periwinkles, jasmines, crane's bills, anemones, lavender, viburnum, hollyhocks and golden rod.

1 Royal Widow Auricula.
2 Dwarf white starry Hyacinth.
3 White Bostamon Narciss.
4 High Admiral Anemone.
5 Rhyven Narciss.
6 White passe flower.
7 White grape flower.
8 The lesser black Hellebore.
9 Danae Auricula.

10 White flowering Almond.
11 Dwarf blew starry Hyacinth.
12 American flowering Maple.
13 Goldfinch Polyanthos.
14 Larger blew starry Hyacinth.
15 Virginian flowering Maple.
16 Narciss of Naples.
17 Best Claremon Tulip.
18 The checker'd Fritillaria.

MARCH

19 Large leav'd Norway Maple.
20 Double pulchra Hyacinth.
21 Queen of France Narciss.
22 Paleo Auri flame Tulip.
23 Blew Oriental Hyacinth.
24 Single bloody Wall.
25 Admiral blew Anemone.
26 Bell Baptice Anemone.

27 Monument Anemone.
28 Red flowering Larch tree.
29 Blew passe flower.
30 Rose Tonker Anemone.
31 White flowering Larch tree.
32 Purple strip'd Anemone.
33 The Velvet Iris.
34 Jerusalem Cowslip.

Design'd by P. Casteels.

From the Collection of Rob.t Furber Gardiner at Kensington.

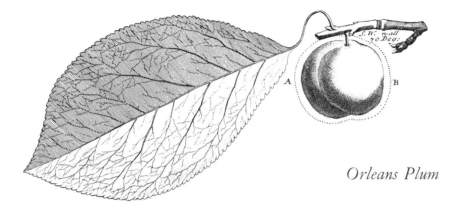

Orleans Plum

...is for Orange Tree Garden

The view entitled *Orange Tree Garden and Rotunda* is one of the eight views of Chiswick gardens by the Flemish painter Pieter Andreas Rysbrack, which were commissioned by Richard Boyle, 3rd Earl of Burlington, *circa* 1729-30. The garden was first remodelled by Charles Bridgeman *circa* 1716, then extended and altered in the early 1720s by William Kent and Burlington, an eminent amateur architect, whom Scipio Maffei described as 'il Palladio e il Jonès de nostri tempi'. Burlington certainly designed the Rotunda, and it is possible that the amphitheatre in which it stands may have been used for theatricals.

Orangeries normally housed the trees in winter and during inclement weather. As the Rotunda would have been too small it is not at all clear where at least seventy tubbed trees would have been stored. Later in the 1730s a new orangery of more traditional form was built on the east side of the garden and this too may have been the venue for theatrical performances. The engraving *below* shows the new orangery drawn by Roque in 1736. An amphitheatrical orange tree garden is peculiarly English, and indeed may be peculiarly Burlingtonian.

Peach

...is for Pheasantry

No other architect or garden designer employed the new and fashionable art of aquatint to such popular effect as did Humphrey Repton, as is shown by his design for the pheasantry at the Royal Pavilion, Brighton *opposite*. Nearly all his gardening books: *Sketches and Hints* (1795), *Theory and Practice* (1803) and *Fragments* (1816), owe their success to aquatint, but none more than the beautiful folio of *Designs for the Pavilion at Brighton* (1806). It was to have been built in the style of Hindustan. Although the Prince Regent promised to 'have every part of it carried into immediate execution', the designs were never used, and the exotic palace that was eventually built at Brighton was designed by John Nash. Repton's pheasantry demonstrates his elegant mastery of this ornamental form of garden architecture. Pheasantries, as well as aviaries, developed from the 18th century menagerie. One of the most famous was the one in Kew Gardens, known also as the Pheasant Ground, where Chinese and Tartarian Pheasants were kept in pens and cages. The Aviary and Flower Garden at Kew engraved by Thomas Sandby is shown *above*. It was designed by Sir William Chambers *circa* 1758.

Quince

...is for Quincunx

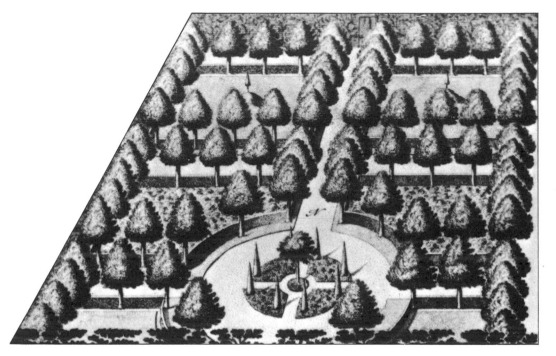

The illustration *opposite* appears in John James's 1712 edition of Dezallier d'Argenville's *Theory and Practice of Gardening*, written in 1709. The quincunx as a pattern is said to have been derived from ancient Egyptian net-work or gnat nets. Xenophon's description of the plantations in King Cyrus's garden at Sardis is the earliest reference to the quincunx in gardening. The agricultural writers of the first century BC and AD writing in Latin give much attention to the planting of trees. One method was to plant five trees in the pattern now found indicating 'five' on a dice. By the Middle Ages the term quincunx was clearly used much more loosely to cover formal plantings of trees. James describes the quincunx as an arrangement of five spaces, or 'cabinets' in the form of an X which is visibly and arithmetically the double of a Roman V. In the quincunx opposite the four corners each with an open space or 'cabinet' would, if seen from above, look like the four corner dots of the quincunx in its strict sense. However, *above* is a so-called quincunx in the garden of St. John's College, Oxford, from William Williams' *Oxonia Illustrata*, 1733 and it is difficult to relate this pattern to the earlier idea of a quincunx.

A Wood planted in Quincunce with Cabinets

A Little Hall invironed with Palisades & green Borders.

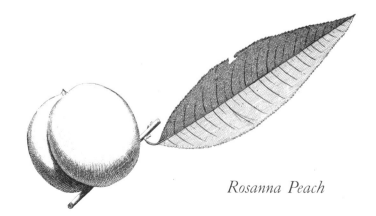

Rosanna Peach

...is for Rosary

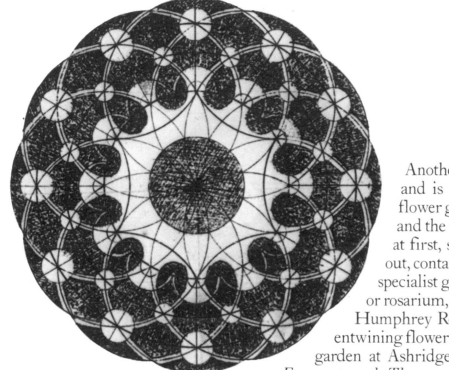

Another beautiful aquatint by Humphrey Repton is shown *opposite* and is of his own Rosary at Ashridge Park, Hertfordshire. The flower garden belonged particularly to the age of Repton and Loudon and the Gardenesque in the early 19th century. Flower gardens were, at first, simple parterres, but soon more complex gardens were laid out, contained within a walled or paled area and divided into a variety of specialist gardens: an American garden, an arboretum, a grotto, a rosary or rosarium, as well as a flower garden proper. The rosary was favoured by Humphrey Repton who always enlivened it with decorative treillage and entwining flowers. His most famous rosary was the one incorporated in his new garden at Ashridge Park. Descriptions and aquatints were published in his *Fragments on the Theory and Practice of Landscape Gardening* in 1816. This was very much the age of ornamental gardening and the prettiness that gardeners and garden architects created was somehow reflected by their reproduction in the colourful and attractive art of aquatint.

Above is a design for a geometrical rosary by the astronomer Thomas Wright, laid out in the 1740s for Lord Barrington at Becket Park, Berkshire.

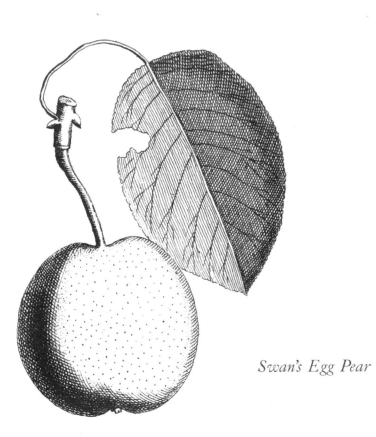

Swan's Egg Pear

...is for Seat

Opposite is a seat by Walter H. Godfrey which was illustrated in *Gardens in the Making*, 1914. But there have always been seats in the garden: even in medieval gardens there were simple benches. In Tudor gardens, seats were transformed into arbours and the idea of the covered seat persisted until the 18th century. During the 1730s and 1740s, the age of the rococo, seats reached a peak of fantasy and complexity of design. More than any other age, it seemed to be that of activities in the garden. Thomas Robins' ravishing gouaches can be explored for an extraordinary variety of seat patterns, especially Windsor chairs and settees. Other seats are of more severe architectural form, and at garden entrances stand porters' chairs propped up against trees. The porter's chair *above* was drawn *circa* 1755 at Woodside House, Berkshire, while the tree seat *below* was in the gardens of Sir John Gibbons' Stanwell Place, Middlesex, *circa* 1750.

The Victorians on the whole preferred cast iron furniture, and this too could be of inventive design, but tended to be stereotyped in pattern. There was a revival of 18th century forms of furniture in the Edwardian years, especially with architects such as Lutyens and garden designers like Gertrude Jekyll.

Tawny Fig

...is for Tent

The design shown *opposite* for a Turkish tent is by Henry Keene and probably dates from the 1750s. When Mrs Lybbe Powys visited Stourhead in 1776 she remarked of the Turkish tent there, 'tis of painted canvas, so remains up the whole year: the inside is painted blue and white in mosaic'. There was also a Turkish tent in Vauxhall Gardens, another at Pains Hill, Surrey, and one at Belle Vue in Ireland. Such tents were ephemeral, and none of this type has survived. Copper tents survive at Haga Park, Sweden, designed by J. L. Desprez in the 1780s. Also at Haga is a Turkish tent pavilion built by F. M. Piper, almost certainly with the Stourhead tent in mind, for not only did Piper make a detailed study of Stourhead, but the Haga tent likewise had a blue and white interior.

The Venetian tent *below* is from John B. Papworth's *Hints on Ornamental Gardening*, 1823.

...is for Umbrello Seat

An Umbrello'd Seat.

Opposite is a design for an umbrello seat by John B. Papworth. Umbrello seats were sometimes called parasol seats and in their most simplified form resembled an open umbrella. It was an obvious adaptation to a garden seat or resting place from the middle years of the 18th century onwards. It became a Regency fad. This seat was proposed by J. B. Papworth in his *Rural Residences* of 1832 as an 'embellishment to the lawn or shrubbery', being of the 'marquee character'. Papworth had earlier proposed such tent designs in his *Hints on Ornamental Gardening* of 1823. The umbrello seat *left* is from Charles Over's *Ornamental Architecture in the Gothic, Chinese and Modern Taste*, 1758.

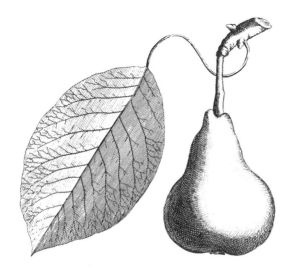

Vermillion Pear

...is for Vegetable Garden

The Practical Kitchen Gardiner:
Or, A New and Entire
Syftem of Directions
For his Employment in the
MELONRY,
KITCHEN-GARDEN,
AND
POTAGERY,
In the feveral Seafons of the Year.

Being chiefly

The OBSERVATIONS of a Perfon train'd
up in the Neat-Houfes or Kitchen-Gardens
about *London*.

Illuftrated with PLANS and DESCRIPTIONS
proper for the Situation and Difpofition of
thofe GARDENS.

To which is added, by way of SUPPLEMENT,

The Method of Raifing CUCUMBERS and MELONS,
MUSHROOMS, BORECOLE, BROCCOLI, POTATOES,
and other curious and ufeful Plants, as practifed in
France, *Italy*, *Holland* and *Ireland*.

And alfo, An Account of the LABOURS and PROFITS of a
Kitchen-Garden, and what every Gentleman may rea-
fonably expect therefrom in every Month of the Year.

In a METHOD never yet attempted.

The Whole Methodiz'd and Improv'd,

By STEPHEN SWITZER,
Author of the *Practical Fruit Gardiner*.

—— *Et quas Humus educat Herbis*
Fortunata fuit. —— Ovid Metam. XV.

LONDON: Printed for THO. WOODWARD, at the *Half Moon*
over-againft St. *Dunftan's* Church in *Fleetftreet*. 1727.

Opposite is a detail of Thomas Robins' painting of Charlton Park, Gloucestershire, showing the vegetable garden.

Montezuma's garden contained only medicinal and aromatic herbs – and was typical of medieval and early Tudor gardens where the kitchen garden was planted with herbs rather than vegetables. Montezuma thought it not kingly to cultivate utilitarian plants near the house, and his vegetable or kitchen garden was sited a distance away. By the late 17th century in England, the kitchen garden had been brought near to the house once again, and in Kip's engravings of Knyff's views of country estates, plots of vegetables and fruit feature as importantly as the parterres and pleasure grounds. As the 18th century progressed the kitchen garden was moved away again and given a special walled area, often a great distance from the house. However, although this might be the case with great estates, squires' remote domains, like Charlton Park, have remained unchanged through the centuries since the late Middle Ages.

The two illustrations on this page come from two books on the practical aspects of gardening. *Above* is the title page from Stephen Switzer's *The Practical Kitchen Gardiner*, 1727, while *below* is a plan of a vegetable garden from Batty Langley's *New Principles of Gardening*, 1728.

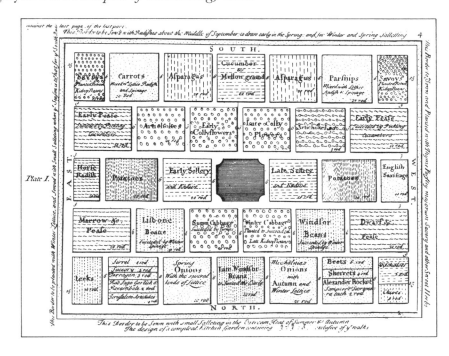

Windsor Pear

...is for Water-works

The water-works built by Thomas Bushell at Neat Enstone in Oxfordshire were perhaps the most remarkable of any in the 17th century. Thomas Bushell was known as the Enstone Hermit and belonged to the mystical world of Renaissance hermeticism and such astrologers as Dr John Dee. The curious Enstone water-works were regarded as wondrous devices to accompany the hermit in his solitary contemplations. Robert Plot in his *Natural History of Oxfordshire* writes in 1677 that Bushell 'laid divers Pipes between the Rocks, and built a house over them, containing one fair room for banqueting, and several other small Closets for divers uses'. These were shown to Charles I on 23rd August 1636. For the King's pleasure, 'there arose a Hermit out of the ground, and entertained them with a speech; returning again in the close to his peaceful urn'. Bushell obviously had fun for he was keeper of the water-works 'that turns the Cocks by way of sport to wet the Visitants of the Grot'. When John Evelyn visited Enstone on 22nd October 1664, Bushell had two mummies in his grotto and 'lay in a hamoc like an Indian'. Evelyn also remarked on the 'extraordinary solitude' of the place. The small water-work on the island was an addition made by Lord Litchfield, of nearby Ditchley Park, when he repaired Bushell's old water-works in 1674.

TAB.XI. ad pag. 137

...is for eXotica

The fishing temple at Virginia Water *opposite* was drawn by S. S. Teulon in 1860, and an earlier drawing by William Delamotte of the temple and its flower garden was made in William IV's reign, and is shown *below*.

Exoticism became an enduring element in English gardens after Richard Bateman lived the life of a pseudo-mandarin in the early 1730s at his house at Old Windsor. The centre of the craze for exotica was Kew Gardens where the House of Confucius, the Pagoda, the Mosque and Alhambra were built in the period from 1749 to 1760. In 1753 John Haynes had drawn and engraved the Duke of Cumberland's Chinese yacht, the *Mandarin*. This sailed on the lake in his park at Virginia Water, which when it later became one George IV's favourite retreats, was ornamented with chinoiserie buildings as exotic as any at Kew, and amongst which was the fishing temple. In 1826 Lady Holland

noted that the new temple was 'in the Chinese taste, full of gilt dragons for ornaments,' and her comment that it was 'rather too expensive' is borne out by its cost – over £2500. Sir Jeffry Wyatville certainly built it, but Frederick Crace, the decorator of the equally exotic Brighton Pavilion, was the designer and artist. The King enjoyed fishing here or dining in the house or one of its flanking tents. Most surprisingly, S. S. Teulon, one of the rogue architects of the Victorian age, restored the temple in 1860.

The Fishing Temple · Virginia · Water

The · Central · Building · shewing · the · Style · of · Decoration

proposed · for · the · Entire · Exterior

This is the Drawing referred to in
my Contract dated August 13th 1840.

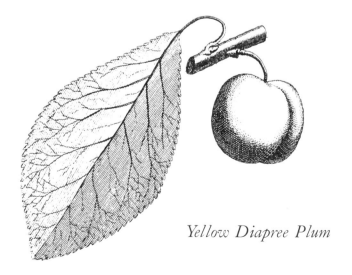

Yellow Diapree Plum

...is for Yew Topiary

The yew exedra at Hartwell House, Buckinghamshire, painted by Balthazar Nebot in 1738 *opposite* was perhaps the most fantastic part of the extraordinary theatrical topiary garden at Hartwell House. As this painting is dated 1738, the yews must then have been well over forty years old. So this is a topiary garden of the reign of William III. Although Dutch and French influences can be detected, the way the garden is put together is essentially English. Just as little is understood about the influence of fortification manuals upon French formal garden design, even less is known about the sources for gardens in the theatrical style. At Hartwell, one section of the garden was laid out with yews cut into vistas simulating shutters on a stage.

Below The complicated art of topiary could hardly be better illustrated than by this sheet of patterns copied, perhaps by Henry Wise, from *'Yews at Versails'.*

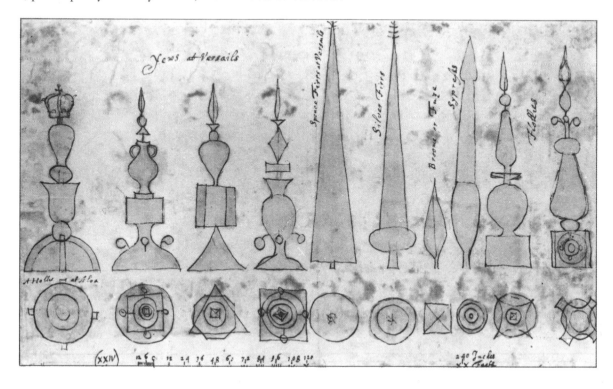

Zantoyne Grape

...is for Zoological Gardens

Opposite is a lithographed view of the Emu House in Regent's Park in 1831.

The Zoological Society of London was founded in 1826, and was established from the beginning in the Regent's Park Gardens. It was perhaps inevitable that Decimus Burton, John Nash's co-architect for much of Regent's Park, was consulted about the new Zoo right from the start. From June 1826 he was busy designing and building and was formally appointed Architect to the Society in 1830. The first Zoo was planned in the tradition of pleasure gardens like Marylebone, Vauxhall, or Ranelagh, but with the animals contained in temples and ornamental buildings. This followed continental practice as at the *Jardin des Plantes* in Paris. To commemorate the completion of the first stage of building, James Hakewill published *A Series of Ten Views of the Southern Portion of the Gardens of the Zoological Society in the Regent's Park* in 1831, with a second issue in 1834. Nearly all of Burton's work has been destroyed, but fragments remain of the Raven's Cage, the Clock Tower and the Giraffe House. Fortunately his East Tunnel of 1829 survives almost intact.

This page shows lithographed views of the monkey house in Regent's Park.